WHAT'S
HAPPENING
TO

Confession

?

By Leonard Foley, O.F.M.

Nihil Obstat:

    Rev. Hilarion Kistner, O.F.M., S.T.D., S.S.L.
    Rev. John J. Jennings, S.T.D.

Imprimi potest:

    Very Rev. Roger Huser, O.F.M.
    Provincial

Imprimatur:

    +Paul F. Leibold
    Archbishop of Cincinnati
    April 14, 1970

Cover designed by Lawrence Zink

SBN 0-912228-00-8
Library of Congress Catalog Card Number: 79-132545
©1970 St. Anthony Messenger Press

Printed in the U.S.A.

Contents

Introduction

We take so much with us into the darkness of the confessional! So many memories of past confessions and matters so personal that we may never discuss them elsewhere.

For some of us these past confessions are a happy memory. We remember pouring out our shame over a sin now admitted in all its evilness, telling of our worries or crosses to a confessor who really listened. He seemed to understand our sin or problem and by his acceptance and warmth made us feel God's mercy and forgiveness and strength. We left relieved, peaceful, hopeful, confident that we had met Christ and He had touched and healed us.

For others, the memories are painful. Maybe the trouble started way back with the fear of a child for dark places or the mistaken torment of an innocent soul over having done "bad things." Maybe it started later when scrupulous memory was tortured by the worry that "serious sin" (childish curiosity and play) had not been confessed adequately and therefore for years "bad" confessions had been made. Maybe our uneasiness with confession arises from the searing memory of a priest who did not at all understand our problem or showed impatience or anger or lectured us harshly for a weakness we could not seem to overcome. Perhaps the coldness of the setting, the haste of the confessor, the pressure from teachers or parents to "get to confession," the terrible routineness of our recital of sins, have left us emotionally sterile, although convinced in faith that our sins are forgiven. Maybe we left the box not relieved at all but worried about whether we had told *all* our sins, whether we had mentioned all the aggravating circumstances and whether we were really sorry for the right motives.

But whether confession is basically a consolation or a dreaded ordeal for us, it has played a major role in our understanding and practice of Catholicism. Confession, like fish on Friday, was one of the things that made us different from our Protestant neighbors.

Even if it has been an experience we dreaded and avoided, we are startled when someone starts tampering with it. When the lines grow shorter and articles sound alarm, we wonder if confession is going the way of rosary and Benediction, novenas and the quiet Mass. We feel uneasy when we think sacred practices are no longer carried out and revered with the fervor of old.

Then pop up the worries: Have we been given the wrong word on confession? Did we sweat through telling all of our sins for nothing? Are the laws still as strict or is it OK now to tell less? Must I still insist that my children go to confession frequently? What is it that the young priests and the new theologians are teaching about confession? What has Vatican II said about it?

Maybe without too much conscious reasoning as to why, we find ourselves going to confession less often than formerly. Maybe we always tended to put it off, as we delayed starting a needed diet, but now we are wondering if putting it off is not really OK. Maybe the necessity of confession and the need for regularity were overstressed. Do I really need it that much and that often?

This book tries to answer these questions. It will put confession in the perspective of faith. It will try to convince us that there is no intellectual basis for fears and worries. It will attempt to wipe out the negative elements in our attitude and reinforce the positive ones. Perhaps, as far as written words are able, it may be successful in calming upset feelings and emotions.

In March, 1965, under the editorship of Fr. Leonard Foley, O.F.M., *St. Anthony Messenger* published a special issue on Confession. It was enthusiastically received and reprinted in several different forms. Reprints are still ordered and subscribers write that they have saved that issue because it was such a consolation to them.

The lead article of that issue was entitled,

"Are These Your Worries About Confession?" Its purpose was to clear away the obstacles, the doubts and fears, so that the reader could with untroubled mind and peaceful conscience be open to the positive and beautiful statements about the real nature of the Sacrament of Penance.

In case some of these doubts still plague any of the present readers, we briefly list again:

FACTS FOR THE FEARFUL

1. God's mercy does not depend on your remembering your sins.
2. You must confess mortal sins only according to your present ability.
3. You have no obligation to confess any doubtful sin.
4. No matter how many mortal sins you forget, they are all forgiven.
5. You must confess the number of times you committed a mortal sin only as far as you can reasonably recall.
6. Details of sin should never be confessed— only the specific name of the sin, and circumstances that put it into a different category.
7. If you are trying to be sorry enough, then you are sorry enough.
8. If you're afraid you'll sin all over again, you are normal.
9. If you are now determined to use God's help

to change things, you need not worry.
10. You are not obliged to confess venial sins.
11. You are not obliged to confess the number of times you committed any venial sin.
12. The greatest fact of life is: God loves you, personally, as you are, now.

Our hope is that all of us are now ready to rise above fear, and drive out a preoccupation with ourselves by focusing on Christ and His mercy. This is an entirely new treatment embodying the insights of today, but the basic truths are the same that we were taught, as children or converts, from the Baltimore catechism. But we hope by climbing the mountain to get an overview of these truths. From that perspective we can see confession as a part of God's master plan of love. We will see ourselves as members of a forgiving and forgiven community. The climb to the vantage point demands some intellectual exertion. Trying to get the whole picture stretches the mind. We think the view is worth the effort. Once you've been to the mountaintop, things in the valley look different.

—*Jeremy Harrington, O.F.M.*
General Editor

Chapter I

What's Happening to Confession?

the confession lines—at least the long ones —have all but disappeared from the Catholic Church. A greater percentage of Catholics receive Holy Communion every Sunday than at any time, it would seem, in centuries. But they no longer feel the need of weekly, monthly, sometimes even annual confession.

What has happened? Only the patient research of the sociologists of religion will ultimately give a clear answer. But on the surface it would seem that the following changes of attitude have taken place.

In the great explosion of facts, events and opinions that characterizes our times, some of the reasons why people went to confession have lost their force: 1) a sense of fear (often unwarranted) that they were not worthy to receive Communion unless they first went to confession, even if they were guilty of no mortal sinfulness;

2) a sense of external order that saw great value in certain regular practices of religion—now being questioned as to meaning, purpose, value; 3) a certain docility to those who urged them to go frequently—priests, Sisters, parents—now de-emphasized in the quest for healthy independence of judgment and personal responsibility; 4) some would say that many have lost a sense of sin. It is impossible, of course, to make this judgment about any person. What would seem to have happened is that many people realize that some things they "thought" were sins were not in fact sinful, even by the "old" definition of sin; and they now feel that they "have no sins."

At any rate, much of the formerly existing motivation for "going to confession" is gone. Insofar as this is a step away from fear and misunderstanding, of course, it is a healthy development.

But to say that we will now "drop" confession in the Church is a little hasty, to say the least. Hadn't we better take another look at the whole picture of the Church? What does it mean to "celebrate" the sacramental acts of Christ and the Church, as we are urged to do by Vatican II?

This book attempts to see the sacrament of Penance in the perspective of the whole meaning of Christ and His Body, the Church; in the perspective of the real meaning of sinfulness and God's forgiveness; in the light of every man's personal relationship to Christ and to his fellow-man.

New Emphases, Not a "New Religion"

What's happening to confession, then, *should* happen to it. It is being rediscovered at the heart of the Christian mystery. But a lot of jungle-like overgrowth will have to be cleared away before it can be experienced in its full richness.

This book, in fact, will take a long time to "get to confession." But the "getting there" is all-important: "getting there," first in the sense of clearing away misconceptions, and second in the sense of realizing those Christian fundamentals without which confession is meaningless.

May we begin by pointing to several emphases that are being made today. Please note that this is not an attempt to condemn the past or to say that no emphases like these have ever existed before.

First, there is today a great concern for what is interior to man: call it meaning, sincerity, value or whatever. Externals are essential, but they are not enough.

Secondly, there is a great emphasis on depth, totalness, completeness. Perhaps this is another way of saying "whole soul, whole heart, whole mind, whole strength." A sinner does not change just one little aspect of life: conversion, penance is a matter of total attitude.

Third, there is great concern for the personal. My sins are my unique choice, nobody else's. There is no remedy for them in a book. The personal "me" must use mind and heart in deep awareness and decision.

3

Confession must be seen as a response to God's total love for us.

This means a deeper realization of what faith is: a deep, personal, across-the-board, commitment to God in Christ, a total way of life. From such awareness and experience of personal love of God, sinfulness is seen in its true evilness. We are each individually responsible: no one can sin for us, no one can make us guilty of sin; no one can tell us we have sinned, no one can tell us we have not.

This is another way of saying that man is free, and what he does humanly is done freely. Confession is not a magic box from which comes a certificate of acquittal; it is a free seeking of the healing of Christ. It is not an injection of assurance for emotional anxiety; it is the free admission of real guilt and the glad acceptance of Christ's freely given healing.

Finally, there is a great emphasis on fruitfulness or real change of life: real healing and reconciliation that shows in personal relationships.

These emphases are in the air in both Church and world, and confession is inevitably affected by them—and for the good.

Some Fundamentals of Christian Faith

The trouble with taking something apart is that it ends up dead and useless. We may remove and fully understand a carburetor, but unless it's put back correctly with all the other pieces in the car, it is useless. So there is danger in spiritual matters of considering pieces and saying all that needs to be said about each one, and ending up with nothing but the confusion of a pile of separate pieces.

We will try a different method, that of the artist, who puts a touch here, a touch there, never finishing one element of the painting, but working on the whole at all times. We will try to do this with several elements involved in this topic.

1. *The Mystery of Evil.* We need confession because there is evil in us and in our world. Christian hope is optimistic, but it is not naïve. Christ has overcome sin and evil, the devil, suffering and death. But we are still "on our way" with Him, and the attacks of evil still are felt by the Body of Christ. St. Paul uses the phrase "mystery of iniquity" as the reverse of the "mystery of salvation." The devil, the cosmic evil in the world, has his own plan for the destruction of all that is good. This evil is seen abroad in the world —in hate and cruelty, injustice, and in man's blasphemous self-seeking.

And each individual man knows the evil he has freely allowed to enslave his own attitude, in whole or in part. He knows himself to be selfish, mean, vindictive, self-centered, self-indulgent, uncaring, untrusting, unloving, closed. Even apart from his own real sinfulness he feels the constant pressure of evil upon his mind and heart.

2. *The Faithful, Saving God.* Man sometimes learns his lesson: that he is not God. He cannot save himself from the evil he has allowed to poi-

son his life. *He cannot create his own salvation. He cannot be anything by himself.*

One of the basic facts of life is that man is a creature, which means he is basically one who *receives*: life, the healing of life, the growth of life, the happiness of life. Once he stops feeling humiliated by this, he has already received the greatest of God's gifts: the freedom to accept God's love. God does not create man, see him fall into inescapable evil, and then dare him to win his freedom. God leaves man free, but He remains the faithful God who will never desert man, no matter what man does. He respects man's freedom—otherwise man would not be man—but God is faithful. His love is steadfast.

3. *Salvation, Healing, Forgiveness.* Man finally realizes that being saved is a gift of God always offered, but impossible by human effort alone. God offers every man, at the heart of his person, the *power*, the Spirit, His own life and love, in order that man may be freed from evil. God extends His powerful hand to man to free him from his selfishness and lead him to a trusting love of Himself and open relationship to other persons. Man receives the power to be free, to be happy, to be like God—by receiving from God the power to forgive, to love, to trust, to be concerned, to care, to be open to the needs of others. This is salvation, and it is offered to every man God ever made. Whether that man has ever heard of God, or Christ, or the Christian body, he has within him an awareness of a choice: he can choose good or he can choose evil. Even after

8

choosing evil, he can still receive the gift of God's mercy and choose good. God wills to save him.

4. *The Appointed Savior.* God was not content with meeting every man in an invisible way. The Eternal Word was made flesh. The name "Christ" means He was anointed, *i.e.*, appointed, chosen, empowered, to be savior (Jesus). God so loved the world—the world of man, sinful men, (us)—that He literally gave His Son to save it. He joined a human nature to His own Person, and He plunged Himself into the life of man in all its damaged condition. He could not share man's sinfulness, but He did share the miserable lot which man's sin had brought down upon Him—hatred, mistrust, slander, selfishness, prejudice, pain, frustration, death. And so Jesus was the *Salvation of God*, He was the mercy of God made flesh and living among us.

How did Christ save us? Not by magic. Not by doing something instead of us. He saved us by giving to His Father, at the heart of sinful and hopeless mankind, a perfect human love. He was faithful to His Father. In the worst of our ills, He did not waver: He loved the Father, trusted, obeyed, gave Himself in every situation.

Because of this perfect love in the God-man, the Father gives every single man on earth the power to be victorious over the evil inside him and outside him, by being united to this mystery of Jesus: the so-called Paschal Mystery.

5. *The Paschal Mystery.* The Passover was the central fact of Israel's history. God saved them

by their passover journey from slavery in Egypt to the freedom of a new people, His very own, joined to Him by covenant blood. He saved them, and He would be faithful to them. Every year they celebrated this Passover.

Christ is our Passover. He Himself plunged into the waters of death and then victoriously rose out of them, conquering them—as the Jews had passed through the sea. He has the power to give us the same victory over death and the life of God. The Paschal (*i.e.*, Passover) Mystery is everything that happened from the Last Supper to the Resurrection and exaltation of Christ. It is called a *mystery* because it is, paradoxically, a way of revealing God. It is an event, an act of God done to save man. It is a sacrament of Divine Love.

Our salvation—the salvation of the world—is the applying of the Paschal Mystery to every man. It means that every man can be saved—and God wills that he be saved—by being joined to this saving action of Christ. Man is united to Christ's attitude, spirit, willingness, obedience, trust. To have this divine life, to be one with Jesus' perfect love of His Father, is to be joined to His complete victory over death and sin, evil and suffering and unhappiness.

6. *The Paschal Mystery Today*. Christ came in a human nature—in flesh and blood. He was visible. He talked and walked, ate and drank, because He was for men and He was a real man. He spoke to people, and they loved Him. They did not yet know they were loving God when

11

they responded to Jesus' offer of kindness, forgiveness and hope. But this man who was God was the sacrament of God. He was a sign who made God personally present. To be a friend of Jesus was to be a friend of God, and to have an unbelievable life—eternal life—within one's person. Jesus gradually revealed the mystery. The men and women who freely received His love were to be His body after He was gone. How would mankind know who and what Jesus was? They would know by observing the love and faith of His visible body—the assembly (Church), the gathering visibly of those who had received His life, who had given their faith to Him, who believed in Him and gave Him their lives.

They became members of His body by being plunged into His own Paschal Mystery. They joined Him in death and resurrection through the going into the waters of baptism and the rising to a new kind of life, being made new creations of God, possessed of the very life of God and the Spirit of Christ. Now they in turn are to be the sacrament, the sign, of Christ—they are to show the goodness and power and victory of Christ to the world. They are to proclaim the Good News.

7. *The Sacramental Acts of the Church.* Jesus remains in His Body, the Church. He is *present*. His Paschal Mystery is made present by the sacramental actions of His Body, the Church. When His body, the community of love in His Spirit, acts in His power, men are reborn, they are united in Eucharistic love, worship and meal:

and—to come finally to the sacrament of Penance—they are reconciled after desertion, they are healed in the lifelong battle against evil.

God still comes to the heart of every man. But He wills that all men come to Him through the Body of Christ. If they do not hear of or recognize the Body of Christ, of course, they are saved by the gift of God's love to their own heart. They are saved by the love of Christ, too, even though they are not yet aware of this fact. But it is the will of God that all men be saved by being united in the Spirit to their Brother-man, Jesus. In other words, God communicated Himself as perfectly as He could to mankind, in order to give mankind His happiness. It is not a question of whether or not this was necessary, whether God could have saved us another way. The fact is that God loved us so much that He literally wanted to become one of us. Obviously this added nothing to Him. It was entirely for us—and this is the greatest revelation of what love is.

So it is not a question of some kind of arbitrary arrangement that God wants us to come to Him in Christ. He wants us to come to Him in Christ because that is where He is most visible to us. And this visibility is most present today in the Christ-actions of the Church called sacraments, done in faith and love.

8. *A Particular Sacrament* is a sign-symbol that has present in it what it symbolizes. A husband back from Vietnam rushes to embrace his wife; this embrace and kiss is a sign that already con-

tains and makes visible the love that is already there. This would seem to be a good comparison for the sacraments. They are, as someone has said, signs of life: life already there in God, now given to men. They are signs of love present and now made visible. In the case of confession, it is a sign of healing love now made present and assured.

So, any sacramental action of the Church is an action—a symbol—that happens in some place, some time, which makes visible an invisible reality that is already present—the love and healing of God, in Christ, for those who believe in Him.

9. *Confession.* Remembering what was said above about understanding confession as the artist paints a picture, we should perhaps stop for a moment and ask ourselves if we cannot begin to see that confession is a much more wonderful reality than we have sometimes made it; that the center is Christ, not ourselves; that it is a gift, not an ordeal; and that it is an organic part of a whole life in Christ.

Questions for Discussion

1. What are some of the reasons suggested for less frequent reception of the Sacrament of Penance? How valid do you think these reasons are?
2. What were some of the false fears and misconceptions that some Catholics had and have about confession?

3. Are there signs of real evil in our world? For example? What does St. Paul mean by the "mystery of iniquity."
4. What evidence is there from the Bible that God does not merely leave the sinner to his own misery but forgives and helps?
5. How did Christ go about saving us? Did he "buy us back from the devil"?
6. What is the significance of the Passover for the Jews?
7. How can you as an individual be touched by the Paschal Mystery?
8. What is the invisible reality of which a sacrament is a sign?

Chapter II

What is Sin?

Confession is about sin. More importantly, it is about God. Our understanding of sin will depend on what we think about God. Until we really believe that God so loved the world as to give His only Son to save it, we will not understand sin.

God opens Himself to us in love, and gives us the freedom to open ourselves to Him in response. If we receive Him, we receive life—divine, human, dynamic, eternal life.

The nature of God is to love, to live in the "giving-receiving" relationship of Father, Son, Spirit. God wants to be with us, too. He literally wants to have a relationship of friendship and love and fatherhood with us. "God's will," so often misunderstood as a huge mold into which life is squeezed, is simply that we personally and freely receive His holiness, happiness and life.

He wants to embrace every person in Christ, to have one family forever.

Sin is personal refusal of life. It is man saying No—silently by omission or actively by choice—to God's plan to create him into His own likeness. It is man closing up to the offer of friendship. It is a turning away from God's offer of personal union. It is a rearranging of values by man, independently of God.

It is a closing up in the face of another man's pain, or weakness, or begging for bread. It is a turning away from Christ's request to forgive the person who hurt us, from His desire that we seek to heal rather than punish. It is *using* people—their fears, their hopes, their bodies, their trust—to further an underground kingdom of our own, not openly in conflict with the kingdom of God, but consciously contradicting it. Sin is ignoring the evidence, the truth in others' statements, the justice that cries to be served, the honesty of opinion we know that reality demands. It is putting up barbed wire defenses against the invasion by others' needs.

It is a refusal to grow, to be created, to develop. It is the perverse acceptance of a stunted, drying-up life. It is a denial of reality; for the greatest reality is God's loving personal presence in reality—in every relationship between persons. Sin is the ignoring of God visible in Christ and in His brothers and sisters. The ultimate judgment will be: "I was hungry and you did not give me to eat."

Evil is not *something*. It is what is missing,

what ought to be, for fullness, health, happiness, the overflowing joyful life God wants to share with us. Sin is the opposite of love. It is the refusal to be at one with God and others. To sin is to be unwilling to return the healing of God in the face of indifference or hatred. It is ultimately a refusal to be concerned about God or man. It is selfishness.

Sin is man's declaration of independence from God. To sin is to say, implicitly: "I, too, have a plan; it is to satisfy myself and to make everything in my life serve this plan."

Sin is the refusal of healing. It is not just the refusal of God's primary offer of life. It is the unwillingness to accept God's forgiveness and restoration of life. It is closing the door to the only one who can heal. It is supreme arrogance, reducing the Mystery of the Eternal to a bothersome beggar at the door.

"As Long As I Don't Hurt Anyone"

The deepest mystery of sin is that it has to do with others. No man, indeed, is an island. The very excuse man uses to salve his conscience: "It's OK as long as I don't hurt anybody"— reveals the nature of sin. Every sin is a denial of what I ought to give to others.

For man, to *be* is to *be with*. Even God lives in a relationship of three persons. It is impossible, physically, emotionally, humanly, to be alone and self-sufficient. We need each other, and real life is fulfilling the deepest needs of each

19

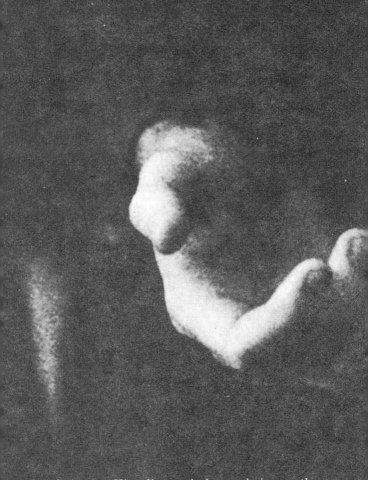

"God opens Himself to us in love and gives us the freedom to open ourselves to Him in response."

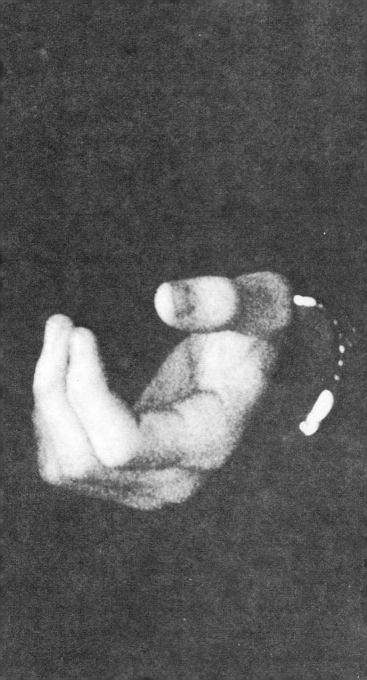

other. The deepest need everyone has is to be loved, and God has sent every man to be His sacrament of concern for every other person. To live, to be human, to be divine, to be Christian, is to be with others for their good. To refuse to do this is to sin, to bring about the absence that is called evil. The most "private" of sins is a poisoning, to one degree or another, of one's ability to be part of the human family. It is a closing up, a hardening, a turning in on oneself.

Someone may object that this is a too-idealistic way of presenting morality. Life is cruel, and people are not trustworthy. You have to defend yourself. There are limits to what you can do for people, and what you can be expected to do. It is enough to give everyone what is *just*, their rights.

There are limits, indeed. Only God can care for everyone at once. But what is *just*? What has every man a **right** to? He has, from the God who made him, the right to be treated as God's own son. "I was hungry, and you did not give me to eat."

In any case, sin spoils the relationship long before the limit is reached.

Bible scholars are pointing out the unsuspected wisdom of the Genesis story. It portrays paradise as relationship: peaceful union of God with man, and of human being with human being. The author expressed this beautiful relationship by saying that God walked with man in the cool of the evening. And Adam exclaims of his wife: "This at last is flesh of my flesh!"

This person is so like me that she is part of me. "And they felt no shame in front of each other," trusting each other.

But sin destroyed the relationship with God, *and they know it*. They hide, in fear and shame. They have destroyed something in themselves that reveals their nakedness before God. And inevitably they destroy their relationship with each other. "It was the woman you gave me!" Adam excuses himself. And when man loses respect for God, he is no longer his brother's keeper. He can refuse a peaceful relationship and descend even to murder. Like Lamech, he can demand 70-fold vengeance. And so "the thoughts of man's heart fashioned nothing but wickedness all the day long." The final result was Babel: every man against his brother. Sin is the wilful spoiling of my relationship to God and therefore to man; to man and therefore to God. "I was hungry and you did not give me to eat."

The Sin That is Mortal,
or Death-Producing

Growth is gradual, not explosive. Our life is a process of becoming. We can become more and more filled with the Spirit of God and grow into deeper awareness of His presence, greater openness to His love, and closer communion with all the members of His family on earth. Or we can become more and more estranged from Him.

Man makes a deliberate choice—usually very gradually—which goes to the roots of his being.

Every man with a mature mind knows he must sooner or later make a choice which affects his whole life.

There is something in him that sums up his whole life, that faces up to the ultimate: an attitude, a basic life-choice. He may express it a hundred ways, but it gets down to one thing. He either chooses, *as a way of life*, that which he knows to be "good," supremely important; or he chooses, *as an overall attitude*, that which he knows to be a denial of basic goodness.

It is a yes or no to the whole moral order as such, and ultimately to God. He may express this in different ways. He may or may not be explicitly aware of God or Christ or law, but he knows what he is doing. What he does has something *final* about it.

If this basic option or attitude is choosing "good," he is responding personally to God's offer of life. If he knows Christ, this is the surrender and commitment of faith. If he knows only "God" in general, it is still the obedience of a total person. Even if he knows only "good," it is the total receiving of the proffered gift of love from God: it is what has been called "baptism of desire."

If on the other hand man *at the core of his being* refuses God, he puts himself in the condition and attitude of being completely and voluntarily cut off from God, and therefore from life. It is an attitude so deeply rooted in his person that the relationship of love with God is destroyed. His wound is mortal and self-inflicted. He is dead, by his own choice.

A Gradual Process

It takes time for love to grow—or die. "Love at first sight" is not the love that endures through the years. So also, man's relationship with God is not finally broken unless it has been gradually weakened. The process ultimately culminates in an attitude that affects the core of his person. It is basic, and what is basic does not easily change—for good or ill.

There are many ways in which the basically sinful attitude can be expressed; but as an attitude, it is simply mortal sinfulness—singular, not plural. It affects a man's whole life, because it affects the core of his being. It is a broken relationship, which is a state of affairs that simply *lasts*. It is not just a set of things that can be isolated, enumerated, "out there."

Christ spoke of blindness, hardness of heart. Mortal sinfulness is self-induced blindness, hardness of heart gradually and wilfully chosen. The rigidity of death.

Then What About the Lists of Sins?

An action—any action—may or may not be the expression of the basic choice just described. There is no way of knowing from the outside. Christ forbade us to judge the guilt of others.

Hence, in teaching the three requirements for

*"God's notion of confession is celebration.
It is a gift, not an ordeal."*

mortal sinfulness, we can never separate the seriousness of the matter from awareness, realization, decision that is full and deliberate. Sinfulness that is mortal arises from the depths of a person. Certain things are so wrong in themselves that they cannot be done with full awareness and decision without destroying one's basic relationship with God—if this is the realization. No action of any given person can be presumed by others to express this awareness and decision. If the person is turning away from God in this action, then his sin is *mortal*. His sinfulness, at the core of his being, is indeed fatal. Otherwise, the action remains one which *in itself* is seriously wrong, as things are described and dealt with *from the outside*. A man may be found guilty of a crime—an external action—without necessarily being guilty of mortal sinfulness.

Some things are right, some things are wrong. One can go to the other extreme of concentrating only on the fact that sin involves personal choice. As human beings we have bodies, we speak words, we use things. Our relationships are expressed in externals, and our intentions can never be divorced from these externals. Part of the virtue or sinfulness of our actions lies precisely in our realization of what our external actions express *of themselves*, and our responsibility for what they do to others, in spite of any "not wanting to hurt" on our part. By cheating in a civil service exam, I may not *want* to hurt anyone else, but I *am* by unjustly depriving a more competent person of a job.

What Then Is Venial Sin?

We have been talking about basic choice, an attitude that comes from and expresses the core of our being. It is evident that not all our actions or decisions, either good or bad, express fully the core of our being. We may have made a deep personal choice for God—and yet some of our actions do not express that love at least in a complete way. They may be *somewhat* selfish. In spite of a morning offering they may not in fact express love of God or man. But the deepest commitment of our person is not thus expressed.

Thus, one who is totally turned away from God may exhibit a certain surface amiability with others with no intention at all of changing his basic attitude of alienation from God, and, for all practical purposes, from man. And one who has truly surrendered his life to Christ in deep faith and love may still be guilty of selfishness that is truly evil, unkindness that is truly sinful, but not the kind of total choice that comes from the depths of the heart.

Perhaps the following comparison will help. Husband and wife, or two friends, love each other deeply—a basic life commitment. One would give up life, if need be, for the sake of the other. And yet, these two are capable of spoiling their relationship *to a degree*. Not to the point of unfaithfulness or separation, but *somewhat*.

Our nature, in other words, may not be completely under our personal control as much as we would (by basic choice) wish. Our nature in this

29

case is all we *are*—all our habits, impulses, feelings—the "what" that God is gradually transforming into a truly free and happy person.

We always fall short of the fullness of love. Our relationship with God and with our fellow human beings is never all that it ought to be. This is venial sinfulness. It has many expressions, and it is important to consider these externals. But again, it is an attitude, one that is simply somewhat-selfish. (If I am willing to hurt somebody, how I do it is a secondary consideration. The evil is in the willingness.) It is a relationship in which we hold back a little—but a little that real love would give, not an extra. We do not really carry out our basic love of God. We do things that are in fact contrary to it. We love our friends, but we find it possible to hurt them a little, by word, or act, or omission. "In many things we all offend."

The Evil of Sin

It is necessary to "talk about" sin as we have been doing. But the very fact of doing so, objectively and dispassionately, as if we were examining the X-rays of cancer in a total stranger, can build up a shield around the horror of sinfulness.

There are some who think we Catholics, Christians, the world, have lost our sense of sin today. Perhaps the explosion of publicity has hardened us to the fruits of sinfulness that cover the world like a polluted atmosphere—war, poverty, racism, the degradation of sex, the built-in injustice, the tragedy of dope and alcohol, the loneliness of all who are not loved—man's inhumanity to man. Perhaps it has all become a "political" problem. Am I my brother's keeper?

A certain amount of faith is needed even to read the signs. A certain amount of love is needed to feel remorse over even serious injuries inflicted on another. The more deeply two people love each other, the more they feel the pain of regret over the little things they do to each other. But when this no longer causes the offender himself to suffer, love has already begun to grow still; it flows sluggishly at best, and the pain now is that of dying, not of being born.

We can see so many war dead that we forget these were persons, born of human beings and destined to live in God forever. And we can become so accustomed to the pollution-presence of evil in the world that this "mystery of iniquity" becomes, like some holy signs, a mere external, signifying nothing.

It all depends on how we see the deepest reality: the presence of God offering us His love, His life, and His eternal friendship. What we do not value, we can lose without pain. We ignore those we do not love. We cannot feel the pain of sinfulness if we do not love the One we shut out.

Questions for Discussion

1. What is the fallacy in the following statement when it is used to justify a sinful act:

31

"It's OK as long as I don't hurt anybody"?

2. In respect to the way he is treated by his fellowmen, what basic right does every man have?

3. Discuss the disruption of the harmony of paradise as a typical effect of sin.

4. What are the alternatives in the basic life-choice that every man must make?

5. What did Christ mean by blindness or hardness of heart?

6. Why is it impossible for us to judge whether or not another person has committed a mortal sin?

7. Can we judge, then, that certain actions are seriously wrong in themselves?

8. How does venial sin differ from mortal sin?

9. Were you taught the correct understanding of sin? Do you think that most Catholics have the correct idea of sin?

10. How do you teach children the correct idea of sin?

Chapter III

Christ Truly
Forgives One
Who Repents

two very important aspects of our picture now present themselves: forgiveness is from *God*; and this gracious God really grants *forgiveness*.

The greatest reality about confession is the presence of the living God. In the light of this fact, anything else is comparatively insignificant —embarrassment, admission of guilt, guilt itself, "doing" penance—all the human things. It is indeed true that God makes us very valuable and worthwhile by His love. But the fact remains: we should think more about God than man.

We are not going through an ordeal; we are not attempting to placate one of the fickle pagan gods. We are not scraping together some human achievements in order to "repay" God for what we have done. We are simply letting ourselves be embraced, like the Prodigal Son, by the all-loving God. As St. Luke describes it, "His father saw him and was moved to the heart. He ran out to him, threw his arms round his neck, and kissed him."

Who is this God? In the Old Testament, He showed Himself to be the God of *steadfast, faithful covenant love.* In the New and Eternal Covenant, He comes in the One who dies to save man.

Whatever the Chosen People did, there was always one unshakable truth: their God would always be faithful. In a daring comparison, it was said that covenant love was the love God showed to Israel His bride, and would continue to show. It is the reason He formed the covenant in the first place. His covenant love is more enduring than the will of man. It is forgiving. Israel can appeal to it when it has sinned. So Moses prays:

"Yahweh, Yahweh, a God of tenderness and compassion, slow to anger, rich in kindness and faithfulness; for thousands he maintains his kindness, forgives faults; yet he lets nothing go unchecked."

And Daniel prays, "Lord, let your face shine again on your desolate sanctuary. Listen, my God, listen to us. We are not relying on our own good works but on your great mercy!" And the prophet Micah says, "What God can compare with you: taking fault away, pardoning crime, not cherishing anger forever, but delighting in showing mercy? Once more have pity on us, tread down our faults to the bottom of the sea. Grant Jacob your faithfulness, and Abraham your mercy." Note what is asked for: faithfulness and mercy.

The prophet Hosea described the covenant between God and chosen Israel as a marriage. God is faithful and He expects from His people the same faithfulness a man wants from his wife. But in the book of Hosea, the wife is unfaithful; yet God, in the action of the prophet, does what no Jewish husband would do: He takes her back. His love does not turn to bitterness or seek revenge but remains constant and unfailing in spite of her fickleness and betrayal. This is the way the forgiving God is described:

"I will heal their disloyalty. I will love them with all my heart, for my anger has turned from them. I will fall like dew on Israel, he shall bloom like the lily, and thrust out the roots like the poplar, his shoots will spread far. He will have the beauty of the olive tree, and the fragrance of Lebanon. They will come back to live in my shade. I hear his prayer and care for him. I am like a cypress, ever green; all your fruitfulness comes from me."

Last of All in These Days

Finally, the kindness and love of God *appeared*. And He said, "The time is fulfilled, and the kingdom of God is at hand. Repent and believe in the Good News." The Good News is that the Father loves us and forgives us in Christ, and gives us His Spirit. We will return later to the forgiveness we receive in the person of Jesus.

37

*"While he was still a long way off,
his father saw him and was moved with pity.
He ran to the boy, clasped him in his arms
and kissed him tenderly." Luke 15,21.*

For the moment let us note that when the apostles went forth to preach the Good News, forgiveness was one of the elements emphasized. "You must repent and every one of you must be baptized in the name of Jesus Christ for the forgiveness of your sins, and you will receive the Holy Spirit. God has raised up Jesus to be leader and savior, *to give repentance and forgiveness of sins* to Israel." "All who believe in Jesus will have their sins forgiven through His name." In this way God makes His justice known: first, for the past when sins went unpunished because He held His hand; then, for the present age, by showing positively that He is just (*i.e.* exercising His saving justice, as He had promised, by just-ifying man, giving him life) and that he justifies everyone who believes in Jesus.

What Does It Mean "To Forgive"?

To forgive is 1) to give up *retaliation*, revenge, an eye for an eye. But God cannot possibly retaliate, *i.e.*, merely hurt us because we hurt Him; 2) To give up *resentment*. God is not like man. He cannot be resentful; 3) To give up *recompense*. What did we take away from God that He could ask compensation for? We did not love Him. We did not accept His life, His coming to us, His help, His happiness, His goodness in Christ. But by His own decision, He has no choice but to keep on wanting us to accept His goodness. In this way, He does demand "recompense." His forgiveness is His faithfulness—

He wants us now to accept the love that previously we refused to accept.

Satisfaction? Penance? Doesn't all this let us "off the hook" rather easily? Shouldn't there be some suffering of punishment, and some purification of ourselves, some making ourselves worthy?

In Catholic theology, satisfaction is the effort, given by God's grace, to make reparation to the goodness and holiness of God for our sins. Common sense as well as faith tells us that this requires some self-discipline: whatever is necessary to change our sinful attitude and keep it changed by whatever natural means we can—including some reasonable self-punishment as a reminder of what we have done. But this is not the making of satisfaction. Only Christ can make satisfaction for our sins, and He does this by His free act of obedience and love. This act—His life, death and resurrection, His perfect attitude—is freely accepted by the Father as reparation for the honor and love of which sin deprives God. Christ does this as the representative of all humanity. So our satisfaction means being joined to the reparation of Christ: His perfect love and obedience.

In other words, no matter what negative turning away and conversion is involved, penance, satisfaction, reparation must ultimately be acts that proclaim and acknowledge the holiness of God and show Him honor and love, in Christ.

Another way of saying this is: God does not

change; His offer of love and healing is always before us. His love simply *possesses us again* when we, by the gift of His grace, turn back to Him in faith and loving obedience. We allow life to flow into us again; or, in the case of venial sinfulness, we allow the return of the *degree* of love that was lost.

The central fact, then, is: God never changes. His will is to be with us, to fill us with His life and happiness. This is not a good-natured indulgence that implies that sin is of no consequence. This love "cost" God His only-begotten Son's death. "God did not spare his own Son, but gave him up to benefit us all". It is not God's saying that sin never happened, or that no damage was done, or that no healing is necessary. But in the end it is the Father of the Prodigal Sons hurrying down all the roads of life to meet and embrace His children. *His* notion of penance is celebration. Should it not be ours?

Repent and Believe the Good News

But what does man do, in this great act of God's mercy? He *receives* the power to respond freely and sincerely to God's love, and he does respond.

It may be good to remind ourselves of two extremes, both false: one holds that on his own, man makes himself worthy; the other holds that nothing really happens inside man: he goes through certain rituals, certain external actions, and by some sort of magic he is "forgiven."

St. Peter's words quoted above speak of God "*giving* repentance" through Christ. And Micah the prophet asks God to "*grant* your faithfulness." It is so easy to come to God in self-sufficiency that we must constantly remind ourselves that "we are not qualified in ourselves to claim anything as our own work; all our qualifications come from God." "No one can say 'Jesus is Lord' unless he is under the influence of the Holy Spirit."

But man does have to say it, in his heart. Central to all Jesus said was the need for deep internal conversion. "Repent and believe the Good News" meant *metanoia*, a change of heart and mind accepting and embracing the good news as the loving gift of God.

We have seen that mortal sinfulness is a gradually developed attitude that goes to the core of a man's life. So also must be his "conversion." In the case of venial sinfulness, the conversion obviously must go as deep as the sin.

Fr. Charles Curran, in an article "The Sacrament of Penance Today," says:

"*Metanoia* is a change of heart which is illustrated in many ways by the New Testament: *e.g.* the passing over from death to life. from darkness to light; the creation of the new man in Christ Jesus; the new life received from the life-giving Spirit of the risen Lord; the joyful return of the prodigal to the house of the Father. This change of heart affects all the multiple relationships in which man finds himself; in fact, this change of heart is known and manifested above

all in man's relationships with his fellow man.
The follower of Jesus is told that he should not
offer his gift at the altar if he remembers that
his brother has anything against him.

"Forgiveness cannot be a merely legal or juridical reality; it involves a profound change of
heart which must manifest itself in the mani-
fold relationships of the Christian with others.
. . . The forgiveness of sin can never remain an
isolated religious phenomenon apart from the
daily life of the individual."

When is this sorrow "perfect" and when is it
"imperfect"? The terms are perhaps not the best.
What is meant is this: God's love overcomes
man's guilt by bringing man to love Him freely
in return. This involves two things: First, the
sinner considers the fact that God's holiness
must demand the rejection of the sinner. God
does not have to "decide" this—it is simply a
fact. Light and darkness cannot co-exist. So the
sinner is moved to turn from sin as offensive to
God's goodness and holiness. (This has sometimes been called "imperfect contrition.")

Second, when contrition reaches its fullness,
and becomes real love of God for His own sake
(either through the sacrament of Penance or before the reception of the sacrament with an ex-
plicit or implicit desire for the sacrament) so
that this love does indeed turn man away from
sin, we speak of "perfect contrition." What matters most is that the "disillusioned sinner be
freed by God's grace from the tyranny of some
good thing without which life seemed unbear-

able, and for the sake of which the sinner was prepared to defy even God's will" (Karl Rahner).

This is God's gift. God takes the initiative. Conversion is the result of God's mercy and forgiveness before it can be the result of man's efforts. Man of himself can never overcome the separation and alienation, which is what sin really is.

What we confess, basically, is our need to be released from the hold that sin has over us. We kneel down before Christ and express our helplessness. Forgiveness is liberation. Confession is placing ourselves, weak as we are, within the power of Christ, and letting His loving presence possess us again—or, in the case of venial sinfulness, more fully.

Repentance, then, should concentrate on God, not on myself. It comes out of a deep understanding that sin is an offense against God's love, "the grieving of the Holy Spirit of God." The sacrament is the meeting of the love which repents with the love which has been offended.

Again, what of "venial" sin? We have seen above that "in many things we all offend." Our deep and basic commitment to God is contradicted by numerous acts of selfishness and neglect, uncharity and pride. So there is need for continual growth and conversion. One of the answers to the present problem about "confessions of devotion" will have to arise from each person's realization of the sinfulness that is still present in his own heart, and therefore, in his relations with others. Penance, then, is a "laborious baptism."

As Fr. Duane Weiland says in a beautiful little book on confession entitled *Resistance*, sinfulness is like the cold of winter. Something must constantly be done to counteract it. This uncomplaining resistance to evil is the reality we celebrate in the sacrament of confession.

Again, "venial" sinners. Fr. Karl Rahner's words may help us when we feel that "good" people really don't need confession. "Each time we must bring ourselves by prayer and contemplation to the appalling insight that of ourselves we are quite unable to break with what we really should repent of, the dreadful mediocrity that has become second nature to us; that our conscience can no longer summon up an honest protest against it. Only if we are painfully made to see that we should be better—but really do not want to be; that our slowness is never really frailty but plain lack of love, can we cry from the depths: 'Help me, even though I really do not want you to help me, because I fear your grace, because it might demand more of me than I would willingly give.' Only then are we able to repent—of ourselves, not merely of our wretched faults."

Questions for Discussion

1. In the Old Testament how did God show His forgiveness of His people?

2. What figures of speech did the Old Testament writers use to express God's love?
3. What is the meaning of *satisfaction* in Catholic theology?
4. In what sense does God demand recompense of a sinner?
5. Strictly speaking, can we make satisfaction of our sins? Why or why not? If we can't, who can?
6. Regarding man's part in forgiveness, what are the two extremes to be avoided? What is man's true role?
7. How does God's love overcome our guilt?
8. Why is confession important for the person who has no more than venial sins to confess?

Chapter IV

The Heart of the Sacrament: Meeting Christ Personally

It must be evident by now that we cannot "solve" the problems of confession by a single answer. It is not just confession, or sin, or sorrow, or the Church, or forgiveness or sacrament. It is all of these things, and more. In the end, there is one "part" of the sacrament that is infinitely above the rest: THE PERSONAL CHRIST.

Whatever else confession is, it is a personal meeting with the forgiving Christ in faith. If we are aware of this, all problems become relatively unimportant. If this is not foremost in our minds, we are in danger of playing with magic.

Christ, the Sacrament of the Encounter With God. This heavy sentence was the title of one of the very valuable books of the last 10 years, written by Fr. Edward Schillebeeckx, O.P. The book simply hammers on a simple fact: Christ is God made flesh. God became visible so that we could see Him: He became touchable, hearable, findable: "sensible" in the meaning that He can be found by our senses, a sensible sign.

Christ not only used signs—water, wine, bread, words, touches—He is the Sign of God. When Christ touched a man, God touched a man. When Christ handed the apostles the bread that was His body, GOD handed the apostles bread that was His body. If Christ spoke to you— *speaks* to you—God speaks to you.

Christ is the way God wants to encounter all men. God does indeed reveal Himself to man by the truth and goodness that every man is aware of. It is true that I can pray to God in the forest, and meet Him in the depths of my heart. But God *did choose* to meet mankind most perfectly in Christ. If I do not hear of Christ in my lifetime, it is no fault of mine: I will be with God. But God wants to come to me visibly in Christ.

So, Christ is the Sacrament of God, His living, visible Sign. (We will see, in a moment, the second great truth implied in this: The Church is the Sacrament of Christ.) God loves us, God approaches us, and God reconciles us to Himself through Christ. *All* men are saved through Christ, whether they know it or not. But God does want all men to know it, and to come to Him through the Way, the Visible Way, the Living Sign, the Sacrament of God. God forgives us through the humanity of Christ. The continual forgiving act of God is linked with the human activity of Christ. The love and mercy of God become visible and real for us in Christ.

(It is almost impossible not to go on and consider the fact that the Church—the visible community of persons who are joined to Christ—continues this visible activity of Christ today.)

We have no doubt that Christ is truly present in the Mass. There is a real presence of His body and blood, soul and divinity. But we find it difficult to *see* Christ personally acting in the other sacramental acts of the Church also, and this is one of the fundamental problems of confession.

The recent Council emphasized "By his power Christ is present in the sacraments, so that when a man baptizes *it is really Christ Himself who baptizes*" (Const. Lit., 7).

Who is this personal Christ who comes? He is God bringing mercy in human words, human love, human acts—of *Christ*. Even as we insist on the personal presence of Christ, we must be careful not to make Him merely an "officially" present Christ. He is present with all the love of God directly and personally offered to us.

He is the victorious and glorified Christ, risen up out of all the pain of human life and lifting us up with Him. He has gone through our pain, even our weakness, our human limitation, our death. Now He comes in supreme mercy to share His victory and happiness with us.

"Mercy" has a beautiful derivation: the Latin word for "mercy"—misericordia—means "pity from the heart." God has a heart for our misery, and the heart is human: Christ. As He

51

was on earth, He comes to us now, with all the eagerness, the intense desire to heal, the tenderness and understanding, the tact, and consideration, the frankness and firmness. He is the sign-sacrament-symbol of God's embracing love.

"Simon Peter, do you love Me?" Fr. Bernard Haring compares our sacramental meeting with Christ to the meeting of Christ and Peter after the resurrection. Earlier, Peter had been the first to "confess" that Christ was the One sent by God, and Christ praised Peter for the gift he had received. This corresponds to our "confessing" Christ by our faith, our basic act of giving ourselves to Christ at the core of our life.

But Peter—and again we see ourselves—had not kept faith. (Whether or not his sin was "mortal" as we have discussed it above—a decision reaching to the core of his life—is none of our business. It is impossible to determine. A kindly opinion would hold that Peter's betrayal was like many of ours.) While being led by the soldiers, Christ looked at him: Christ the visible mercy of God. And Peter was sorry at the core of his person. But he also knew that he was forgiven; by God's gift, God's constant love had flowed into his person to replace what sin had destroyed. Peter "confessed" his sin.

If ever there was a sacrament of confession, this was an instance of it. And what we might call the second half of the sacrament came in the visible and personal encounter of Peter with Jesus after the resurrection. Christ said to Peter, "Do you love me?" and Peter three times "took

back" his betrayal and "confessed" the goodness of God in Christ. This is the heart of the
sacrament of confession: God offering to us reconciliation and healing and our accepting it in
Christ.

Christ says to us, "Peace be to you, my
peace I give you!" just as He did to Peter and
the other apostles and disciples when He appeared to them the first time in His risen life.
Peace is order, sin is dis-order. Christ comes to
transform us gradually into a real likeness of
Himself. He comes to transform our hearts so
that our attitude is His attitude. He continues
creating the new man of baptism—or even brings
him back to life altogether.

He joins us to His own passing-over—His
Passover or Paschal death and resurrection. It
was the spirit and attitude and willingness in
Christ that was valuable in the sight of His Father—the love that nothing, even suffering and
death, could diminish; the trust that no trial
could shake. Christ comes to join us to this
"mystery" or sacrament, so that through visible
signs of reconciliation and love we may be truly
those who have "passed over" with Him to God's
own life and His own human attitude. This is the
positive glorious salvation He came to give to all
who want to accept it.

The saving presence of the suffering and
death of Christ is present to us now. The saving
presence of the rising of Christ is present to us
now. Christ comes to us personally and visibly.
How?

The Church is the Sacrament of the Meeting With Christ

God came to the world visibly in Christ. We have no trouble believing that. But what then? Was His "visibility" important for only 33 years? Was just His mortal lifetime enough, so that a privileged few could deal personally with Him, and the rest of us will have to wait until the end of time? Where do I contact Christ *today?* Or isn't there any need to contact Him personally? If it's enough just to pray to God internally, why did Christ bother to take human flesh in the first place, for a fraction of the world's history? Is His human nature important or not?

If God became man, it must have been terribly important that He become man. And since He has become man, it must be very important for other men to see Him as a man, to be in human contact with Him—visibly.

The answer? The Church is the sacrament of Jesus. If you want to contact Him visibly today, you do so in that visible Body of persons who have been born into a unity that truly shows Him—visibly—to the world. What Jesus was, the Church continues to be. Jesus revealed the Father; the Church reveals Jesus—not just by saying words, but by its *life*, especially its charity in unity.

"This is a hard saying, and who can bear it?" But there is no other way to say it. The activity of the risen Christ today in the world is carried on by His Spirit through the Church; and thus the Church is the sacrament, the living sign that makes present to us the love of God in Jesus.

The Church is not a *thing*, like water, or bread or wine. It is not *that* kind of sign. It is a living sign, as Christ was a living sign-sacrament, of a reality existing within it. In other words, living Christians who come together in faith to visibly form the Church, are a sign to the world of what Jesus is, in His love for mankind.

Who or what is the Church? Before we go any further: the Church is people—men and women, Pope and bishops, priests and sisters, married and single persons—everybody who is visibly joined to Christ according to His will.

One might well understand, from what we have been discussing so far, that the Church embodies the spirit of Christ something as a Negro organization might carry on the spirit of Martin Luther King; or as the communists might show the world the spirit of Lenin; or as Franciscans might carry on the spirit of their founder.

But the Church, the living Body of Christ, does far more than that. Christ is today personally present in His body of persons all over the world.

They become His Body by one of His actions: Baptism. They are made one and sustained by one of His actions: Eucharist. And they are healed of sin and reconciled by one of

55

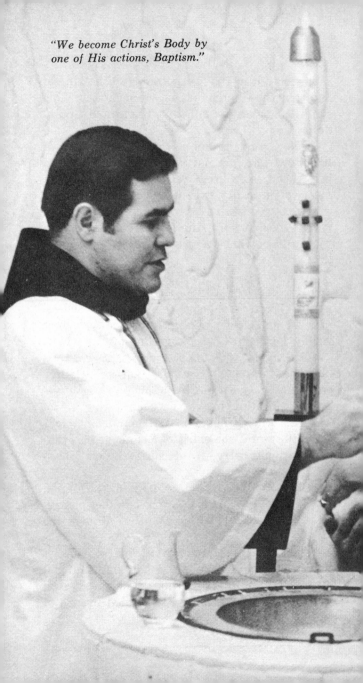

"We become Christ's Body by one of His actions, Baptism."

His actions: The Sacrament of Penance.

In other words, Christ continues to act visibly (sensibly) in the world today through the faith-actions of His Body the Church. The Church is never so much the Church as when she is making visible the "already" presence and activity of Christ in her. To repeat an analogy we used earlier, the embrace of husband and wife on his return from Vietnam makes visible a love that was already present.

The risen Christ, in His Spirit, can approach personally and visibly anyone in the world. He remains visible through the sacramental acts of His Church. This is the marvelous way He continues His Incarnation for everyone on earth—a way that was impossible for His mortal body.

A Catholic confesses to a priest, therefore, because he sincerely believes that he encounters Christ in and through the actions-in-faith of the Church. The priest is a "corporate personality" in this case, that is, he is a representative person through whom the whole Church embraces the penitent. The Church finds a unity in this priest at this moment for this penitent. He sums up the Church's existence in space and time. In him the many are one. And in this "community" representation, Christ the Forgiver acts to reconcile.

The person-to-person meeting with this priest is valuable, as we discuss further. But it is not everything. In the present practice of confession, something has been lost, and the Council has expressed the hope that it will be restored in all the sacraments: the *communal* aspect. The whole Church is involved, and the priest does represent the whole Church, but a celebration of the sacrament by the community would be more expressive of the reality: reconciliation with the Father, through Christ, in His visible Body, the Church.

In other words, if Christ acts through the actions of the Church; and if the Church is the community of those visibly joined in the love of Christ: then these, the greatest acts of the Church, should be evident *community-acts* as much as possible.

We do have this aspect at Mass to some degree; much needs to be done. We have it in a special way at wedding Masses and funeral Masses when a community of people who actually know and love each other join in worship. The new baptismal rite emphasizes parents and community. Parents are bringing a child to a community of believers where salvation is found, by God's will. This baby will belong to a group that has a future, and has hope, and has been *visibly* joined to the saving Christ.

So the substance of the Sacrament of Confession is the Church extending the forgiveness of Christ to an individual on the basis of some evidence of the individual's conversion.

Confession is a making-present of the once-and-for-all sacrifice of Calvary and the victorious resurrection. In this case, it is the making present of the reconciling act of Jesus.

All this depends, of course, on a person's

faith that Christ has in fact given Himself to the Church and has given the Church His power to forgive sins—so that when a person is reconciled with his brothers and sisters who form the Church, he is in fact, reconciled with God. Forgiveness comes through the community of believers, because this community of believers is the sacrament of Christ.

The Church does not merely "declare" the sins forgiven. It makes the saving word of God present and "incarnate" in its sacramental acts. The Church does in fact visibly and effectively continue in space and time the mission of Jesus.

We have lost some of the sense of this "communal-ity", and perhaps that is part of the explanation of the fall-off of confessions. Many find it hard to understand the leaders of the Church saying that even the sacrament of Penance should be as "communal" as possible, as far as circumstances permit. (This is *never* going to mean that public confession of sins will be required!) "Penance services"—to those who have never actually taken part in them—are thought to be some sort of "way-out" togetherness.

But the fact remains: the Church is a community. Its essence is to show the world visible, communal (i.e. brotherly, community, family) love, and by this unity of love to show the world who Christ is and what He wants to give the world.

We are, in fact, Christians because we have been *received into* a visible body. Surely we did not think our salvation depended entirely on a private encounter with a baptizing priest, and that we could then "save our soul" privately, as it were, by saying our individual prayers in a church building, with little or no relationship to other persons who happen to be there doing the same thing?

It's hard to say this: but actually it's because the community allowed us to be a member that we are allowed to take part in the community's sacramental actions. I have to be made a visible member of the visible Body, by Baptism, before I can partake in the community celebration of Eucharist—or confession. We have received, in fact, a participation in the priesthood of Christ.

It Was More Evident, In Other Days

In the early Church, one who sinned publicly was declaring (if it was something serious) that he was choosing not to follow Christ. Obviously, then, he was also choosing to absent himself from the Eucharistic community of those who were following the life of Christ. (Immediately one sees all sorts of difficulties—what about "private" serious sin? How was guilt determined?) When the sinner wanted to be reconciled to the community of Christ, he was required by the community to spend a certain amount of time doing penance before he was readmitted. On Holy Thursday, the Bishop and the community welcomed him back to the visible unity of Christ in the Church. This was the sacrament of Penance, the living sign of Christ's forgiving through His visible community.

It is the same today, though the communality is not so evident, and the healing is extended to all sinfulness, mortal and venial. In confession we are reconciled with God by being reconciled with the community of Christ.

At the Bottom of it All: *Life is Social, Love is Social, Sin is Social*

No man is an island—in love or sin. To be human is to be with other human beings in relationship to them. To be a person is to go out to others in love and receive their love in return. To be is to be with.

We all need some privacy, of course. And sometimes we need solitude. But the greatest punishment man has devised is solitary confinement. Life is other people. If we are with them well, we are fulfilling the purpose of the God Who is Himself three persons in community. If we are with them for ill, then we are sinning. There is no middle ground. I am always in relationship to people. What I am—for good or ill —determines how I treat them. If I am sinful in my attitude, it will affect them.

So there is no such thing as a "private" sin. Sinfulness is my attitude, and my attitude determines everything I do. If I destroy my relationship with God by a decision that goes to the core of my life, I cannot really have a relationship of love to any human being. If I have "only" a venially sinful attitude, it is an attitude, and it weakens everything I do for others.

We don't love each other as a consequence of loving God. We love others with the same act as we love God. To commit mortal sin—to live in the basic decision of mortal sin—is to be cut off from others at the deepest level of life—the grace and love of the Holy Spirit.

Sin fights Christ where He most wills to be —in the relationship of love between God and man, between man and man. And Christ heals this sickness precisely where it is—in the *relationship* of God to man, and man to man. Since man's life is visible, social, communal, He redeems man by saving acts that are visible—the sacramental acts He performs in His visible Body, the Church.

And man, in his being reconciled to God, is also reconciled to his brothers and sisters—the Church which he has wounded by his sins, and which by charity, example and prayer seeks his conversion. (Const. Church No. 11). If we sin— and insofar as we sin—we hurt the Body of Christ, the community of Christians. We are not only *dead*, but we are dead *members*. In the lesser sickness of venial sinfulness, we are somehow thwarting the full flow of Christ's Spirit from us to others by our selfishness, egotism, negligence, and pride. Sin is refusal to love, and therefore, by its nature it disrupts, causes discord, spoils relationships.

Karl Rahner says we each ought to contribute our share to the holiness of the Church by walking in the Spirit. We must make it the holy Church, to witness that God has come. The holiness of the Church is given to the member as his own, and he in turn is to give his holiness to the Church. By sin he offends against her Spirit, her mission, and against the unquestioning obedience he owes her. He makes the Church sinful in a certain way. Even venial sin does this: it forms an obstacle to making God's love actual in man. It diminishes the depth and power of God's love which should be found in a holier Church. Superficiality, lukewarmness, great or small egotism, obstinacy, want of prayer and penance— all these hurt the Church.

Christ visibly-sacramentally present, then, and His Body-visibly-joined in faith are the heart of the sacrament.

Questions for Discussion

1. How could the practice of confession be turned into a sort of magic?
2. When we speak of the sacraments being sensible signs, what does *sensible* mean?
3. What do we mean when we say that Christ is "the Sacrament of God."
4. How do we *visibly* meet Christ in confession?
5. Why does a Catholic confess his sins to a priest rather than directly to God in the secrecy of his heart?
6. Why is it fitting and important that a group

of friends celebrate the Sacrament of Penance together?

7. Why *celebrate* confession at all? Isn't it an ordeal for most Catholics?

8. How does the Church work for the conversion of a sinful member?

9. Name some specific ways that you can contribute to the holiness of the Church?

10. How might one diminish the holiness of the Church?

Chapter V

**Bringing Everything
Into Focus:
This Sacrament,
This Person**

god comes to us visibly in Christ. The same Christ comes to us visibly in His Body, the Church. When we visibly respond as individuals, we celebrate one of the seven sacraments.

"Visibly" (or "sensibly" *i.e.* in a way that can be perceived with one of our senses) is a key word. We are not just spiritual beings, and we do not just lead spiritual lives. To be human, we need both body and soul, acting as one. Hence, our human relationship with God is not fully human unless it is expressed with our whole person, body and soul.

This is not to say that if one is prevented from expressing, say, his thanks to another visibly, he is not grateful. It is to say that if he never expresses his thanks when he can, that he is not truly thankful. It is indeed true that the Spirit of God comes to anyone anywhere, as He pleases. But it is also true that God did come to us visibly in Christ; it is His will that we come to Him through the visible Christ, and through this visible Christ as He remains visible in the acts of His Church. It is true that external actions are worthless if there is no love within; by the same token, there is no love within if nothing is ever expressed.

Fully Human Meeting With Christ

Let us not be thrown off the track with the problem of how often one should celebrate the visible meeting with Christ. Let us just try to see the human value—even the necessity—of sacramental meeting as such.

Psychologists tell us that we partly-spiritual persons grow to personality in and through our body and its contact with the world around us. We express our personal development the same way. This is not just an unwrapping of a package, or the showing of something already fully developed. The bodiliness is part of the humanness. Our external acts may not fully express the reality inside, and to that degree, the reality inside is not fully grown.

To make a very long story very short: if a mother loves a child, she will sometimes put her arm around that child to *show* her love. If husband and wife love each other, this love will sometimes be expressed by word or kiss or embrace. The giver is not satisfied until he gives visibly; the receiver is not satisfied until he receives visibly. So God took us as we are—body-soul persons—and comes to us visibly. We need some kind of sensible assurance of His love and forgiveness. These are the sacraments. Love needs a language of sign. Both the lover and the beloved need it. Faith needs a sign. God gives us His, in Christ. We give ours, in celebrating the visible acts of the Church in Christ and in response to Christ.

The Judgment of Mercy for the Individual

There is another aspect to the "visibility" of the sacrament of Penance. We are not self-sufficient. Our repentance does not forgive our sins —only God forgives sins. Only God can give us the power to turn to Him in penance. This is simply a caution against the oldest and most pervasive heresy of all, that says *we* can put God into our debt, somehow. God's pardon becomes audible in the sacrament of penance—His was the first word, and His is the last word. It is the judgment of mercy in concrete form.

The great benefit of sacramental celebration —whether for "mortal" or "venial" sinners—is the wonder of meeting the act of God's reconciliation visibly and audibly. The word of Christ's mercy is not just "out there somewhere" but it is literally heard in my life. The act of redemption is visible to me here and now.

The sacrament is Christ's expressly taking-hold of us as individuals here and now—as when, in His mortal life, He spoke to *this* man, *this* woman, put His arms around *these* children.

Christ comes to us as individual members of His Body, visibly united with each other. The mystery of His life, death and resurrection is made present. As one teacher expresses it: Christ says, in the visibility of His Body the Church: "Mary (or Joe, or Susie) here is the mystery *for you.*"

Moments When Long-Forming Decisions Are Expressed

The sacraments should be special and culminating moments in life, focusing moments. Most of our life is ordinary. That does not mean it is worthless. But most of the time we are going along on former great decisions (*e.g.* the vocation of marriage or priesthood, paying for a house or car, continuing a friendship) or we are gradually building up to new ones.

At some moment, then, this slowly-formed decision is made external. It is expressed in a decisive moment. I do now sign the contract, I do now join the Marines, I do take the job, I do marry this person. The sacramental actions of the Church are similar. They set the direction of my life. They bring my Christian life into focus here and now. They are moments of renewal of the great decisions that must continue through my life—loving union with Christ and His members in Eucharistic worship, and a decisive turning away from sinfulness.

Our need for the sacraments which can be received frequently (confession and Communion) will be related to our need for a sign of life: God's love and forgiveness visibly joined to my faith and repentance.

We need sacramental activity because the sometimes-intense awareness and appreciation of our relationship with God tends to fade, like all values that are not kept before our eyes. It is true that there may be some interior experiences of our life that are more intense and filled with the experience of God than our sacramental actions. But in the long haul, taking life as it goes, we need the regularity, the visibility, the definiteness and decisiveness of external sacrament.

After the great decisive moments of Baptism, Confirmation, Marriage or Holy Orders, then, and in anticipation of the decisive moment of serious illness, we find ourselves with weekly or daily focusing and decisive re-expression of our faith in Eucharist. And sometimes in Penance.

It is true that Eucharist blots out our daily faults. But it does not take the place of the sacrament of Penance. Penance should precede Eucharist. Eucharist is the symbol and sign of Christ's uniting His Body and nourishing it, and taking it to the Father. It is not primarily the forgiveness of sins that is the concern of Eucharist. We appear as sinners before the tribunal of God in the sacrament of Penance. It is true that all sacraments point to the action of the one Sacrament, Christ. But we need to face Christ precisely as sinners. And we need to meet Him

"*Growth is gradual, not explosive.
Our life is a process of becoming.*"

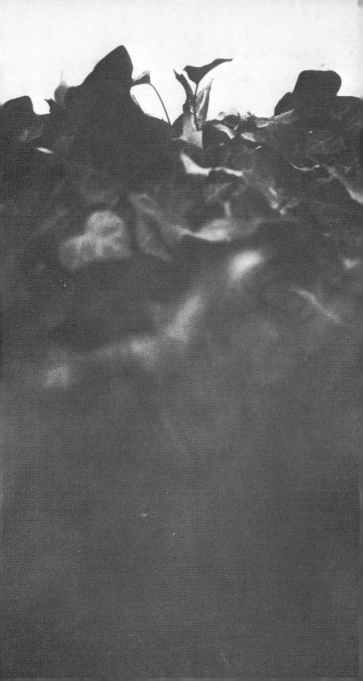

precisely as the One-who-forgives.

Personal Responsibility

In the end, it all gets down to me. Christ became a man, and He talked to individual men and women. The Church is a community of individuals who make decisions and assume responsibilities. Community is not a magic mass of good will—it is individual men and women making the decision to come together in unselfishness and love. But each individual is the key. Everything depends on what he or she holds as valuable, what he or she decides and does, body and soul.

The trend toward emphasizing communality can never mean that someone else—especially a "group"—can take my place, or make my personal confession to God for me. I must face God with personal response. But if I am truly human and Christian, I respond within the community, with Christ, visibly.

The sacramental acts of the Church must be my acts—the Church is people. They must be actions that place my whole life again and again within the life of Christ—or rather, receive the power and spirit of Christ into my whole life.

The sacraments *unite* my life—body and soul, ordinary and "special" times, myself and my neighbors, myself and Christ, sickness and healing, hunger and nourishment, individuality and community, earth and heaven.

The sacramental acts of Christ unite the

parts or stages of my life: growth is by definition gradual. Eucharistic and penance celebrations bring about the gradual refashioning of my attitude so that it becomes the attitude of Christ. This means healing what is sick and evil, and enlivening what is already healthy. Christ comes visibly to liberate us, gradually, from all the causes of sin.

Frequency of Confession

There is no answer to the question "How often should I go to confession?" just as there is no answer to the questions, "How often should I speak to my friend?" "How often should I sleep?" "How often should I pray?" If I have made a basic option to turn away from God at the core of my life—mortal sinfulness—then of course the need to turn back to God is immediate and ever-present. How often I should personally meet Christ the Forgiving Sacrament of God visibly is a matter for personal responsibility to decide. How often do I need to "go" in order to gain a growing revulsion and disgust for sinfulness, selfishness, for all the stunting and thwarting of God's love and energy in my life? How often do I need the self-discipline of again placing my constant and unchanging weakness of temperament ("I always confess the same 'thing'!") within the healing power of Christ? How often do I need something out of the ordinary to keep the ordinary healthy and growing and vigorous?

75

Private Confession

We have spoken about the nature of the sacramental acts of Christ and the Church as *communal*. In the future, it seems certain, the Church will bring the social nature of sin and forgiveness into focus. But this is not to deny the value of person-to-person dialogue in the sacrament. The ministry of reconciliation by Christ was also personal.

In private confession the priest is a "corporate personality" making present the whole Church. (If this is sometimes an imperfect sign, it is nevertheless a sign.) He is a believer, a member of Christ, engaging in dialogue with another believer who wants to talk about his sinfulness, his lack of generosity. The penitent wants to hear something from another believer about God's love for him, about the presence of Christ, about how he can respond with the kind of love and attitude that Jesus Himself had.

And After Confession

In the early Church, penance was done before reconciliation. In confession today, the priest "gives us a penance" which is a symbol of a whole life of penance—a constant turning away from all that is evil, a constant turning more and more simply and humbly to the good God in Christ and in others. We do not make up by our own efforts for anything we "owe." We simply become more and more deeply possessed by the attitude and spirit of Christ. God is interested in the present, not the past. His will is our holiness, now.

In the famous Apostolic Constitution whereby Pope Paul "ratified other forms of penance besides abstinence from meat and fasting," there is a wholesome and unified presentation of what penance should be in one's whole Christian life. Since man is body and soul, penance will always include physical asceticism. But man is body and soul, and hence one must appreciate the whole Christian triad of penance: prayer, fasting, and charity.

The Holy Father points out that the aim of penitence is love and surrender to God. Therefore Christ is the supreme model. Thinking of Christ, then, the Holy Father invites us to accompany inner conversion with the voluntary external practice of penance in these ways: 1) faithfulness to the duties of our state of life; 2) acceptance of hardships arising from our work; 3) acceptance of the difficulties of human coexistence; 4) bearing the trials of life patiently; 5) bearing patiently the utter insecurity of life. Persons with the suffering of illness, poverty, misfortune and persecution are invited to unite their sorrows to the sufferings of Christ, for their own happiness and that of others. And finally, we should join to all this, the Holy Father adds, some voluntary act apart from the renunciation imposed by the burdens of our everyday life, as the example of the saints teaches us.

77

In This is the Love

Life begins with God, and goes to God. God comes to us in Christ, we go to God with Christ. The final purpose of the sacramental acts of Christ and His Church is to worship God. The confession we make is ultimately that of Peter: "Lord, you know that we love you." We confess the faithfulness of God, and the glory of His mercy.

So this is what's happening to confession. We have a long way to go. But the Way is present and visible among us.

Questions for Discussion

1. Is our repentance enough to forgive our sins? Why or why not?
2. What is the greatest benefit of confessing our sins to a priest?
3. In what sense are confession and Communion *renewals* of the great decisions of our lives? What do they renew and how?
4. What might the fact that "I always confess the same thing" indicate to me?
5. How do you answer the question, "How often should I go to confession?"
6. What are the advantages of confession for a person who has no serious sins to confess?
7. What is the purpose of the penance the priest gives us in confession? Why is it inaccurate to think of our penance as "making up for what

we owe" to God for our sins?

8. Using the five ways of practicing penance mentioned by the Holy Father as guides, suggest some practices that could appropriately be given by the priest as penance in confession.

Appendix I

A Brief History
of the Externals
of the Sacrament
of Penance

rom the beginning, the substance of the sacrament has been the application of the Saving Mystery of Jesus to a penitent sinner by a mandated officer of the Christian community, on the evidence of true conversion.

The story of how this application has been made down the centuries reveals a Church greatly concerned with its ministry of reconciliation. At the same time one sees a Church that is quite human, both in the sinfulness that invades its ranks, and in presence of excesses both to the right and to the left. Man seems to have an especially difficult time finding the balance between rigorism and laxity.

One sees also the inevitable influence, both for good and ill, of culture and events. There is the constant battle to preserve the spirit in the letter; and to keep the letter a meaningful expression of the spirit. The stress on communal celebration today is a reaction to the unfortunate decline of the emphasis on the Christian community's part in the administration of the sacrament, as individuals fled from the severity of the public discipline.

The Meaning of Penance in the New Testament

Penance and forgiveness are the very heart of the Gospels. Christ's first words to the public were: "Repent and believe in the Good News!" Penance, or conversion, a complete change of mind and heart from evil to faith and love, is absolutely necessary for salvation and must be permanent. God's love knows no bounds as to the number or kind of sins needing forgiveness. Only when a sinner impenitently hardens his heart—the sin against the Holy Spirit—is forgiveness impossible.

Forgiveness is not a matter simply concluded between God and man—it must come through the mediation of the Church, which has disciplinary power over believers who fall into sin. The Church has the power to "bind and loose."

St. Paul

In St. Paul's letters, there is an insistence on thorough-going conversion. Sin is still a menacing force even in the lives of the baptized, so that no one can feel secure. But not even sinful Christians are lost: Christ pleads for them, and

God's judgment is averted if the sinner is chastised here on earth either by his own hand or the hand of God.

Forgiveness has a churchly dimension: brotherly charity imposes the duty of admonishing one who errs. The severest form of admonition by the Church is excommunication—i.e., severance of relations in the hope that this will finally produce reconciliation.

The Other Epistles

The tension between the Christian ideal of sinlessness and the reality of life is clearly attested. But all sins can be forgiven except the "sin unto death," which is the sin against the Holy Spirit.

The churchly dimension of sin and repentance is seen in the belief that prayer for sinners will be heard. Confession of sins is recommended: a contrite consciousness of guilt, joined to a desire and prayer for forgiveness. James says, "Confess to one another."

The Apocalypse insists that bishops not tolerate grave sins, such as idolatry and unchastity, in their churches; they will be judged harshly if they do not expel such sinners from their flocks. However, the sinners are not lost forever; God subjects them to affliction to bring them to repentance.

At the close of the apostolic period, we see no complete picture of a primitive penitential doctrine and practice. But the main outlines are clear: 1) Every sin calls for penance; 2) no sin, even the gravest, is excluded from forgiveness, provided there is real conversion and penance; 3) prayer and works of mercy are means of obtaining the forgiveness of sins; one's personal prayer receives effective support from the prayer of the faithful; 4) confession of sins is sometimes joined to prayer; 5) rulers of the Christian community are obliged to admonish the guilty and even to excommunicate them to bring about final reconciliation; 6) reconciliation with the body of believers is a guarantee of forgiveness by God.

The Theology of Forgiveness in the Early Church

An early writing (the *Didache*) urges Christians to confess their sins before they pray and to confess their sins to each other before they celebrate the Eucharist. Another writer (Hermas, 140 A.D.), believing the Second Coming to be imminent, speaks of one (and only one) chance for forgiveness after Baptism. God's forgiveness presupposes the doing of penance and reconciliation with the Church.

In the primitive Church, conversion to Christ and baptismal rebirth supposed a commitment that was total. It was expected that grievous sin would be quite exceptional. It seems that the power to forgive sins was infrequently exercised, and the attitude in the Church during the first two centuries was one of great severity. Forgiveness was a "laborious baptism" and was even called a "second baptism."

In the third century two problems arose. First, the problem of those who fell away during persecution; second, the problem with the Montanists, heretics who among other things condemned "lax" practices of reconciliation of certain classes of sinners. The Church can forgive sinners, they said, but will not do so, in order to keep others from sinning. Unforgivable sins were idolatry, murder, and adultery.

St. Cyprian and Pope Cornelius did nothing new in permitting those who had lapsed during persecution to re-enter the fold. What was new was the speeding up of the period of penance before reconciliation with the Church. This was done so that by eucharistic participation they might grow in the strength to resist the temptation to defect a second time.

Orders of Penitents

There emerged a penitential discipline for baptized Christians who had fallen into certain grave sins: idolatry, apostasy, murder, adultery. A penitent guilty of any of these sins was publicly admitted (only once in his lifetime) to a kind of order of penitents.

The *sins* for which one had to be reconciled through the penitential discipline were the four just mentioned. (St. Augustine, writing in the early fifth century, also lists stealing and deception, hatred, participation in pagan spectacles.

St. Caesar of Arles, writing in 543, includes many more.)

There were three phases in the reconciliation process:

1) Entrance into the order of penitents. First, one told one's sins to the bishop privately. Then followed a public liturgical rite of entrance into the penitential discipline. The penitent is designated as such, perhaps with distinctive clothing. In France, one's head was shaved. The penitent is excluded from the Eucharist but not from the community of the faithful.

2) A period of penance. The bishop decided the length of time penance was done, and what penances were to be observed. Some examples of penances: no meat during the time; coming for imposition of hands daily during Lent; wearing sackcloth and ashes; carrying the dead at funerals; long prayers. Monastic influence brought penance into sexuality and extended penance *after* the final reconciliation; for instance, marital intercourse was sometimes forbidden for life; and one was ineligible for the rest of his life to be a merchant, soldier, court official or a member of the clergy.

3) Reconciliation, a final liturgical act before the bishop and the entire Christian community. The liturgical ceremony consisted of a declaration of one's sinfulness and need for forgiveness. No indication is given that the particular sin had to be confessed aloud. The bishop imposed his hand on the penitent as a gesture or reconciliation with the Church, the Body of

Christ, and this reconciliation was a guarantee of God's forgiveness. It was the whole penitential discipline, not just this final liturgical act, which was considered as bringing about forgiveness and the grace of the Spirit. The reconciliation took place usually on Holy Thursday. In necessity, priests could also reconcile penitents.

In the third century, there is no evidence that the Church's ministry of reconciliation was extended in this manner to other signs besides the four mentioned though this did happen later. There emerges only one penitential discipline in the Church at this time. Nor is there any sure evidence for anything like auricular (by ear) confession at this time.

It is to be noted that, at this time and down to the seventh century, satisfaction (or "doing penance") was to be done *before* the final reconciliation. A major development arose when the demands of the penitential discipline grew more and more severe: many simply did not join the order of penitents, preferring to take their chances on being reconciled on their deathbed. There was a parallel dropping off of reception of Holy Communion.

Still another development: the ranks of the penitents were entered by members of the faithful in pursuit of a quasi-religious life—a movement that had some effect on later religious life.

Fourth and Fifth Centuries

The tendency toward mercy—though still

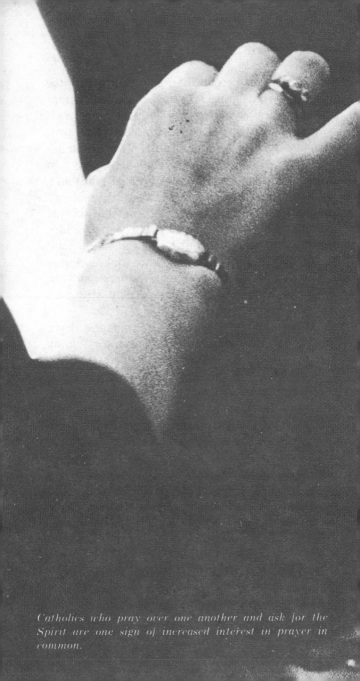

Catholics who pray over one another and ask for the Spirit are one sign of increased interest in prayer in common.

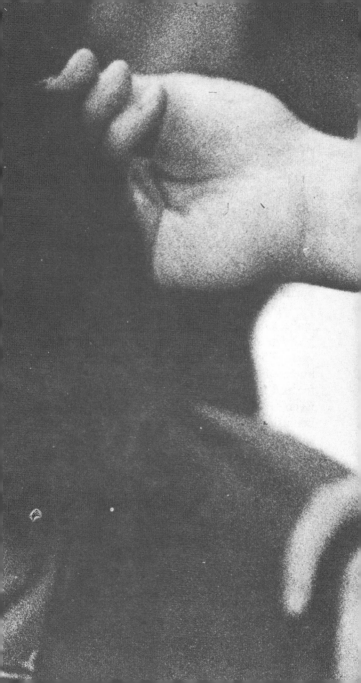

subject to the earlier atmosphere of severity—
began to break through. For one thing, there were
more sinners to deal with. Three factors were
the occasion for defection from the Church—and
consequent requests for readmission: 1) the
Arian heresy, which denied that Christ was God;
2) the Donatist heresy, which among other
things held that a sacrament is invalid if administered by an unworthy priest; 3) the persecution of Diocletian. The mass of these "unreli-
able" Christians who fell away found the penitential discipline of the Church too severe.
Hence, they preferred to avoid the discipline by
putting off reconciliation for a long time.

Thus, there was little recourse to the sacrament, and public penance began to lose its ef-
fectiveness, though it remained solemn and severe. There was an increase in the specified
kinds of grave sins which needed to be atoned
for and forgiven within the penitential discipline.
Even after reconciliation, there were lingering
penalties which the forgiven sinner had to ob-
serve for the rest of his life.

Only those of mature years were admitted
to the Order of Penitents, since Penance was
given only once. There was much writing in this
period against the rigorism of the Novatian heresy, which denied the Church's power to absolve
heretics, idolaters, murderers, adulterers, and
fornicators. There was an attempt to discern the
role of the Church in God's giving of forgiveness.
By reconciliation with the Church, the sinner
was able to return to God. "In this great act,

Christ continually intervenes," says Pope St. Leo the Great. There was some "private" penance in the sense that it was administered to the dying, with relatively little severity.

Toward the end of the fifth century, penitential discipline declined because of the collapse of the Roman Empire and the coming of the barbarians, and the depravity of the Merovingian society. There was still great concern for public penance, and "private" penance was not approved. But the sacrament became less juridical. Satisfaction came to be more and more emphasized during the Lenten season. The majority of the faithful waited until they were at death's door to benefit from the more lenient penance administered to the dying. But there was strong conviction about the need of the sacrament. Some priests administered the sacrament more than once, contrary to episcopal and synodal warnings, such as that of Council of Toledo in 589.

From the Sixth Century to the Thirteenth

There is apparent a growing pressure against public penance: 1) as the emphasis on interiority grew; 2) as the rigor of penitential discipline became harder to bear—the satisfaction required was severe, sometimes lasting for life; 3) as the practice of "waiting till the end" continued. At least one Bishop, Caesar of Arles, encouraged his people to prepare for this penance before death even though they were not able to participate in the public canonical penance of the Church. Fr. Cyrille Vogel, a historian of dogma, concludes: "It is extremely probable that the faithful who, at the exhortation of their pastors, sincerely repented and tried by good works to merit penance at death, were admitted without reconciliation to the Eucharistic table."

Sometime toward the end of the sixth century, and in the seventh, a new mode of the Church's ministry of forgiving sins appeared on the Continent. It seems that the new trend originated in the Celtic churches of Ireland and England. Monks began what would today be called "confession of devotion" in their monasteries. Their spiritual experience attracted laymen eager to find confessors who could give appropriate advice and were accustomed to measuring out penalties in proportion to the guilt confessed. It is now that we have the "Penitential Books" with "tariffed" (i.e. specified) penances. These books indicated specifically what particular penance was called for by a particular sin.

There was a decided contrast between the new and old disciplines. In the ancient canonical discipline 1) only certain sins were confessed; 2) this was done to the bishop; 3) there was a time of satisfaction *before* reconciliation with the church; 4) there was a reconciliation ceremony.

In the new mode of penitential discipline which developed, 1) all sinners approached as often as they wished; 2) penitents addressed themselves ordinarily in secret to a priest, not a bishop; 3) the priest identified the penance for each sin according to the specifications of a penitential book; 4) penitents then left and performed their penances; 5) they returned for final absolution.

Some of the penances prescribed for particular sins by the penitential books were fastings, vigils, bodily mortification, praying the psalms, giving alms, abstinence from sexual intercourse, and pilgrimages.

Sometimes these penances were so severe that they could not possibly be done in one lifetime (like consecutive prison terms today). The result was a system of substitutions or commutations. One could substitute saying the 150 psalms three times for a year of fasting, etc. One could also find a holy person to do penance for one's sins. It takes no great amount of imagination to picture the abuses that resulted from this practice.

In the Ninth Century, as part of the reform under Alcuin, there was stress on confession to a priest and the intervention of the Church and interior forgiveness. Attempts were made to outlaw the penitential handbooks and to revive public penance. But any results of the attempt to bring order into chaotic practice collapsed with the crumbling of the Carolingian empire. Public and private penance overlapped. Since there were many kinds of "penance," there arose a tendency to laxity through the choice of the least burdensome. Attempts were made to "do" three years of penance in one. One story says that a "great man" could complete a seven-year penance in three days by hiring an army of peasants to fast in his place for three days! Some tried to restore the ancient discipline, but it was impossible; private penance became more and more widespread. There seems to have been a new principle invoked: private penance for private sins, public penance for public sins. This was new in the sense that formerly all serious sins fell under one canonical penitential discipline.

Around the year 1000, absolution of sins (the term itself was new—formerly the word was "reconciliation") was given immediately after confession of sins before the penance was carried out.

To sum up, by the 12-13th century, there were three modalities of penance: 1) Solemn Public Penance was imposed for particularly scandalous sins. These were reserved (i.e. for forgiveness) to the bishop and penance was under his supervision. It resembled the ancient canonical discipline. Sinners entered on Ash Wednesday, were reconciled on Holy Thursday. This solemn Public Penance could not be repeated.

2) Non-Solemn Public Penance was for less scandalous sins and could be imposed by pastors. For the most part in consisted of a simple ceremony at the church door (the pilgrim's door) in which the penance of making a pilgrimage was imposed. Pardon was granted upon return, or was given at the place of pilgrimage by "pardoners" located there.

3) Private sacramental confession came from the practice of the Celtic monks described above. This form of penance was open for all men, for all sins, and could be repeated.

Theology of penance began to be developed in the 12th century. All 12th-century theologians were "contritionists," i.e., they gave preponderance to interior contrition. But the question inevitably arose: why confess, if sins are already forgiven by contrition? The first answer given was: to enable the priest to make a sound judgment. The question also arose: Is the confession of sins a divine or ecclesiastical law?

Some theologians said absolution had only "declarative" value—contrition had already forgiven sins. Satisfaction, once greatly emphasized, was seen to be accessory, since it could be done after absolution.

The famous law of 1215, "Omnis utriusque sexus" ("All, of both sexes," i.e. must receive the sacrament) marked a definite step in the history of the sacrament. For grave sin confession was now required once a year, and to one's own pastor. There was far greater emphasis on the importance of the absolution itself. Theologians denied the sacramental nature of the former practice of confessing to laymen.

In very brief form, the doctrine of Thomas Aquinas is as follows: The entire sacrament is the sign and the cause of the justification of the sinner. God's grace begets love in the sinner; he rises from slavish to filial fear. Contrition, perfected by love, wipes out sin. But sacramental confession is still necessary: the virtue of penance and the absolution together form the sacrament.

The Council of Trent

Luther held that the sinner is radically corrupt; he is incapable of repenting. He is aware of this, and is terrified; he abandons himself with confidence to God, who then "imputes" the merits of Christ to the sinner. God then looks on the sinner *as if* he were justified. The disposition of the sinner is one of faith and trust, and this alone forgives. The priest is simply the proclaimer of the Good News when he absolves the sinner. Christ, said Luther, did not intend confession as a sacrament, for it was not possible that out of a corrupt heart, there could come contrition that would obtain the forgiveness of sins; this would do an injustice to the all-encompassing merit of Christ.

The Council of Trent in 1551 taught 1) Penance is truly and properly a sacrament. 2) The absolution is not merely "declarative" 3) There is a distinction between perfect and imperfect contrition. Perfect contrition is that which is made perfect by love of God. It includes the desire to receive the sacrament. Such sorrow effects reconciliation before the actual receiving of the sacrament. Imperfect contrition is that which is motivated by the seriousness, number and disgracefulness of sin, the loss of eternal happiness, and the incurring of eternal damnation. It cannot "justify" (i.e. bring one into the state of grace, because it does not, by definition, include the love of God described in perfect contrition), yet it disposes a man to receive the grace of God in the sacrament. 4) All mortal sins must be confessed, along with circumstances that change the nature of the sin. 5) Confession is necessary and is of divine institution. The secret manner of confessing is not foreign to the institution and command of Christ. 6) Bishops and priests only are the bearers of the power of the keys. 7) Since there are remnants of sin (temporal punishment) remaining after the sacrament, priests have a serious obligation to impose a penance.

The Roman ritual of 1614 prescribed that the priest, in surplice and stole, should receive confessions in the church and in a confessional. Abuses, for which confessors were both justly and unjustly accused, brought the requirement of the grate (screen) in the confessional. The bringing of the sacrament into the church and the privacy of the confessional gave a new solemnity to the sacrament and emphasized, at least implicitly, the respect of worship.

Since the Council of Trent, there has been little development, dogmatically or liturgically, in the sacrament of Penance. Our day is seeing a renewed concern with the communality of the sacraments, the personal activity of Christ, and the primacy of charity in the dispositions of the penitent.

What we see happening today, it would seem,

97

is another chapter in the long history of tensions in the matter of reconciliation: between the necessary internal spirit and the necessary external expression; between severity and leniency; between the authority established by Christ and the freedom of the individual; between habit, custom and past experience on the one hand, and the need for growth, imagination and adaptation on the other; between the rigorist and the laxist tendency; between the call of the Spirit and the drag of not-fully-redeemed human nature; between man's complete dependence on God and his need to be personally responsible.

But history can be reassuring. Christ lets His Church "be"; and for all its falterings and weakness, He is always the victorious Lord of heaven and earth.

Communal Celebration
of the
Sacrament of Penance

One of the purposes of this book has been to emphasize the social nature of Christianity. We are not saved by ourselves alone, but in relationship with others. This relationship, moreover, is not between angels—spiritual beings—but between human beings, body-spirit people who must express themselves in external, physical ways.

Sometimes there must be, therefore, physical-visible expressions of the Christ-life in human beings, and, at the same time, the continuing here-and-now activity of the Risen Christ. The Church is never so much the Church as when it is visible; and it is not visible except when its members are together *as such*.

So the community-sacramental actions of the Church are the highest expression of Christianity. The liturgy, as Vatican II says, is "the summit toward which the activity of the Church is directed."

The Council also said that "whenever rites, according to their specific nature, make provision for communal celebration involving the presence and active participation of the faithful, this way of celebrating them is to be preferred, as far as possible, to a celebration that is individual and quasi-private" (Constitution on the Liturgy, 27).

Obviously, if the public acts of the Church are not really the expression of interior faith and love, they are worthless. But insofar as they at least imperfectly express the desire to follow Christ in brotherly charity, they are eminently human.

In communal celebration of Penance, Christians gather together to express their oneness in Christ and their mutual need both to apologize and to forgive. They express their nature as a forgiving as well as a forgiven people. They listen to the word of God, respond to it with a view to their own sinfulness. They pray together as the Body of Christ that He may heal their sinfulness, increase their love and understanding for each other, and for others symbolically present. And in union with Christ they worship the Father and thank Him for His mercy.

Communal celebrations of the Sacrament of Penance are in their infancy. As time goes on, their purpose will be more clearly seen and appreciated, and the actual ceremonial will become more expressive and moving.

For the present, communal celebrations will

probably be for the relatively few. It is to be hoped that they will always be entirely voluntary.

We are printing an *example* of a penance service below, mainly for an informational purpose. As is evident, nothing is changed as regards the private confession of sins (except that it will usually have to be rather short on this occasion). But the prayers, hymns, and readings attempt to express this community's sense of gratitude for the mercy of God, mutual forgiveness and apology, trust and joy in the presence of the merciful Christ, and a united worship of the Father.

Communal Celebration of the Sacrament of Penance

(The following is *one example* of a form that the celebration might take.)

A) OPENING HYMN

B) EXPRESSION OF SORROW FOR SIN
   Priest: Let us acknowledge our sinfulness, that we may worthily celebrate the sacrament of penance.
   You who were sent to heal the contrite of heart: Lord have mercy
   People: Lord, have mercy
   Priest: You who came to heal sinners: Christ, have mercy

People: Christ, have mercy
Priest: You who sit at the right hand of the Father and intercede for us: Lord, have mercy
People: Lord, have mercy

C) FIRST READING Genesis 3, 1-13 (The fall of man)

D) RESPONSE (*1* indicates half of the group, e.g. the right side; *2* the other half)
(Other forms on page 107.)

1. I acknowledge my guilt, O Lord; I grieve over my sin.
2. O Lord in your anger punish me not, * in your wrath chastise me not;

1. For your arrows have sunk deep in me, * and your hand has come down upon me.
2. There is no wholeness in me because of my sins.

1. For my iniquities have overwhelmed me; * they are like a heavy burden, beyond my strength.
2. For I am very near to falling, * and my grief is with me always.

1. Indeed, I acknowledge my guilt; * I grieve over my sins.
2. Forsake me not, O Lord; * my God, be not far from me!

1. Make haste to help me, * O Lord, my salvation!
2. I acknowledge my guilt, O Lord; I grieve over my sins.

(Kneel for silent prayer)

E) PRAYER (By priest alone, or all together)
O Lord, most kind/ receive us into the loving embrace of your mercy/ and grant us more abundant life./ May the spirit of darkness have no power over us,/ who have been restored by your Son./ May we be cleansed from every act of unloving/ so that we may more readily show our bond of love for one another/ even our enemies./ May this sacramental action of mercy help us to be for others now and forever.
People: Amen.

F) SECOND READING   I John, 1,8 to 2,6 inclusive.

G) SECOND RESPONSE (Other forms of D and G on page 107)

1. O Lord my God, I cried out to you and you healed me.
2. O Lord my God, forever I give you thanks.

1. Sing praise to the Lord, you his faithful ones, * and give thanks to his holy name.
2. For his anger lasts but a moment; * a lifetime his good will.

1. You changed my mourning into rejoicing.
2. You clothed me with gladness, that my soul might sing praise to you without ceasing.

1. O Lord my God, forever will I give you thanks.
2. O Lord my God, I cried out to you and you healed me.

H) SECOND PRAYER

O Lord, God and Father of us all, send the Spirit of your love. Make us see and realize the evil we have done and the good we have knowingly neglected to do; the sinfulness of our attitudes; the full extent of our unfaithfulness in your service; our unfairness and unconcern about our neighbor and ourselves; our failure to keep the basic commandments of love of self, neighbor and You.

People: Amen.

I) HOMILY

J) Community confession of sinfulness in our relationships with others: (Another form of J is found on page 110)
For not really loving my fellow man as I love myself, *Forgive us, Lord Jesus.*
For saying things I know will hurt others, *Forgive us, Lord Jesus.*
For failing to take a stand for the betterment of the poor and needy, *Forgive us, Lord Jesus.*

For disregarding the needs of others when I should have helped, *Forgive us, Lord Jesus.*
For not really paying attention to others when they speak to me, *Forgive us, Lord Jesus.*
For talking too much about myself and not letting others express themselves, *Forgive us, Lord Jesus.*
For failing to try to understand others, *Forgive us, Lord Jesus.*
For my narrowness of interest and disregard of others' opinions, *Forgive us, Lord Jesus.*
For my attitude of selfishness, *Forgive us, Lord Jesus.*
For my failure to really love and accept myself, *Forgive us, Lord Jesus.*

K) Private sacramental confessions are now made to the priest in the confessional. Observing the need for integral confession of mortal sins, we urge very brief statements of sinfulness, of which examples are given in Appendix III.

L) PUBLIC ABSOLUTION TO THOSE WHO HAVE CONFESSED PRIVATELY (if permitted in the particular diocese) The community responds "Amen" to each of the four prayers.

M) COMMUNAL SACRAMENTAL PENANCE (e.g. saying the Our Father together)

N) CLOSING PRAYER

O Lord Jesus Christ, by the shedding of Your holy Blood, You washed away the sins of the world. You then said to Your Apostles: "Whose sins you shall forgive, they are forgiven," so that by the power of that same holy Blood, our sins might be absolved in the sacrament of Penance. Now that you have poured out on us the grace of forgiveness, lead us on to the Kingdom of Heaven: You who live and reign with God the Father, and the Holy Spirit, forever and ever.

People: Amen.

O) Closing Hymn, e.g. "Now Thank We All Our God."

ALTERNATE RESPONSES
(Can replace preceding responses D, G.)

1. Happy the man whose offense is forgiven, whose sin is healed.
2. O happy the man to whom the Lord imputes no guilt, whose spirit is pure.

1. We have acknowledged our sins, our guilt we do not hide.
2. We said, "We will confess our offenses to the Lord."

1. And you, Lord, have forgiven the guilt of our sin.
2. So let every good man pray to you in time of need.

1. The floods of water may reach high, but him they will not reach.
2. You are our hiding place, O Lord; you save us from distress.

1. Rejoice, rejoice in the Lord; exult, you just!
2. O Come, sing out your joy, all you upright of heart.

1. Glory be to the Father, and to the Son, and to the Holy Spirit.
2. As it was in the beginning, is now, and ever shall be, world without end. Amen.

1. Have mercy on me, O God, in your goodness.

2. in your great tenderness wipe away my faults;
   purify me from my sin.

1. For I am well aware of my faults,
   I have my sin constantly in mind,
2. I have sinned against none other than you.

1. You are just when you pass sentence on me.
2. You are blameless when you give judgment.

1. Purify me until I am clean.
2. Wash me until I am whiter than snow.

1. Create a clean heart in me,
2. put in me a new and constant spirit.

1. Do not banish me from your presence
2. do not deprive me of your holy spirit.

1. Be my Savior again, renew my joy,
2. keep my spirit steady and willing;

1. Lord, open my lips,
2. and my mouth will speak out your praise.

1. My sacrifice is this broken spirit,
2. you will not scorn this crushed and broken
   heart.

1. The Lord heals the brokenhearted and binds
   up their wounds.
2. Praise the Lord, for he is good; his mercy
   endures forever.

1. Sing praise to our God for he is gracious; it is fitting to praise him.
2. He heals the brokenhearted and binds up their wounds.

1. Great is our Lord and mighty in power;
2. To his wisdom there is no limit.

1. The Lord sustains the lowly; the wicked he casts to the ground.
2. The Lord heals the brokenhearted and binds up their wounds.

(Kneel for silent prayer)

1. How precious is your kindness, O God!
2. The children of men take refuge in the shadow of your wings.

1. O Lord, your kindness reaches to heaven;
2. Your faithfulness, to the clouds.

1. Your holiness is like the mountains; Your judgments like the mighty deep;
2. Man and beast you save, O Lord.

1. How precious is your kindness, O God!
2. The children of men take refuge in the shadow of your wings.

1. They have their fill of the gifts of your house;
2. From your delightful stream you give them to drink.

1. For with you is the fountain of life,
2. And in your light we see light.

1. How precious is your kindness, O God!
2. The children of men take refuge in the shadow of your wings.

(Kneel for silent prayer)

Another form of J (page 104).
With humble and repentant thought, Father, we confess our sins to you.

We have failed to show your presence in our lives.

We have been indifferent to those whom you have placed in our lives;

We have not tried to understand others and to become one with them.

We have selfishly preferred ourselves to those around us;

We have taken and not given in return.

By sinning against them, we have sinned against your body, the Church, and against you.

Forgive us this lack of love in our lives, as you so often forgave it in those who were so close to you.

110

Help us today and every day in our lives to live in your presence, so that we may be reminders of you to those around us.

Give us the strength to love and forgive so that we may be one even as you, your Son, and the Spirit are one. Amen.

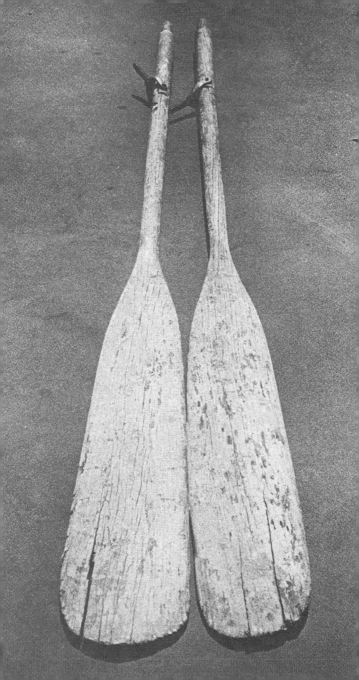

Appendix III

Examples of Brief Confessions of Sinfulness

The following are *fictitious* examples made up to emphasize one aspect of confession—that is, the confessing of *sinfulness as an attitude*. Also, the examples show *characteristic* attitudes, different in different persons. Any *one* of the following examples could be a complete confession, supposing there is no (other) mortal sinfulness. Anyone is free to make his or her confession in any way. But it would seem beneficial to concentrate on one's *particular* and *basic* problem.

"I have been very angry at all my troubles and I let myself be very sarcastic to people I work with, inconsiderate to my wife (husband, children) and uncooperative to people who needed me."

"I am so preoccupied with getting material things and keeping up our status in the eyes of neighbors and associates that I have too little time to talk with my wife and children."

"I let my weakness for liquor lead me to drink too much on several occasions—which in turn led to loose talk, saying many things better left unsaid, lying, etc."

"I take a certain satisfaction in learning and broadcasting the faults of those whose ideas about . . . . I do not like."

"I cause pain and inconvenience to others by thinking of myself first and them second; I am simply thoughtless of others' preferences and feelings."

"I cause inconvenience to others by a sloppy and unplanned way of doing things, making them wait, spoiling their plans, ignoring their needs."

"I realize I am taking a roundabout revenge on others by my remarks about them, even in joking."

"I let my temper or my depression affect my driving and thus endanger my life and the lives of others."

"I am causing trouble in our home by trying to dominate my children, by making all their decisions, not listening to their questions or requests seriously."

114

"I refuse to take responsibility for my mistakes at work or at home. I always find a scapegoat to blame."

"I allow a spirit of bitterness, complaining, self-pity to possess me, and so I don't do others any good."

"I slander public figures, races, religions, classes, by repeating rumors about them."

"I demand perfection in my wife (husband, children) and tolerate no weakness."

"I let profit-getting almost exclusively motivate my business decisions, without giving sufficient weight to the effect this has on other people or the community."

"Because of being preoccupied with many other matters, I neglect visiting my parents."

"I tend to take a selfish view of the opposite sex as a possible means of satisfying my lust instead of seeing them as unique persons made in God's image and likeness."

"I am very stubborn and domineering. If I am blocked by anyone for any reason, I immediately lose my temper and retaliate."

"I continually make myself the hero and center of every conversation."

"I am present at Mass physically, but my participation is half-hearted and spiritless."

"I realize that my mind is closed to any development in my ideas. I don't want to grow in my knowledge of God, the Church, life, myself, or others."

"I show a lack of consideration for other people by habitually being late for meals, meetings, appointments."

"I almost never pray."

"I am somewhat glad when some people have trouble, because it shows them up, and shows how wrong they are in their opinions—which I disagree with."

"I am prejudiced against black persons (Jews, police, young people, liberals, conservatives) and I see everything about them through a filter of prejudice and emotion."

"I have given up on my marriage. It's just mutual toleration now."

"I set my children up for choosing sides between me and my wife (husband) when we are quarreling. I get them to side with me."

"I cause unnecessary pain to my parents by being secretive about my activities and friends."

116

"I show little compassion or forgiveness for the weaknesses of the other members of my family, although I expect them to forgive my faults."

The point of all these examples is that we all have *characteristic attitudes*, i.e., our own particular distinguishing attitudes. And these attitudes have a certain *unity*, i.e., some are basic, and influence our whole life—for good and/or ill. It is *here* that growth and healing are needed most.

ART CREDITS